HOW-TO LIBRARY

CREATING WINTER CRAFTS

By Dana Meachen Rau • Illustrated by Kathleen Petelinsek

CHERRY LAKE PUBLISHING • ANN ARBOR, MICHIGAN

Published in the United States of America by Cherry Lake Publishing
Ann Arbor, Michigan
www.cherrylakepublishing.com

Content Adviser: Dr. Julia Hovanec, Department of Arts Education and Crafts, Kutztown University of Pennsylvania, Kutztown, Pennsylvania

Photo Credits: Page 4, ©Lucidwaters/Dreamstime.com; pages 5 and 29, ©Monkey Business Images/Shutterstock, Inc.; page 6, ©Pressmaster/ Shutterstock, Inc.; page 13, ©Dana Meachen Rau; page 29, ©Monkey Business Images/Shutterstock, Inc.

Library of Congress Cataloging-in-Publication Data
Rau, Dana Meachen, 1971–
   Creating winter crafts / by Dana Meachen Rau.
      pages cm. — (How-to library) (Crafts)
   Audience: Grade 4 to 6.
   Includes bibliographical references and index.
   ISBN 978-1-62431-150-5 (library binding) —
ISBN 978-1-62431-282-3 (paperback) — ISBN 978-1-62431-216-8
(e-book) 1. Holiday decorations—Juvenile literature. 2. Handicraft—Juvenile literature. 3. Winter—Juvenile literature. I. Title.

TT900.H6R38 2013
745.9—dc23   2013010315

Cherry Lake Publishing would like to acknowledge the work of The Partnership for 21st Century Skills. Please visit www.p21.org for more information.

Printed in the United States of America
Corporate Graphics Inc.
July 2013
CLFA13

A NOTE TO ADULTS: Please review the instructions for these craft projects before your children make them. Be sure to help them with any steps you do not think they can safely do on their own.

A NOTE TO KIDS: Be sure to ask an adult for help with these craft activities when you need it. Always put your safety first!

TABLE OF CONTENTS

Time to Celebrate…4

The Winter Holidays…6

Symbols of the Season…8

Basic Tools…10

Ribbon Wreath…12

Oversized Dreidel…14

Kwanzaa Garland…16

Magazine Trees…18

Frosted Snowflake Mirror…20

Light-Up Lantern…22

Foil Wrapping Paper…24

Noisemakers and Confetti Cannons…26

After the Holidays…29

Glossary…30

For More Information…31

Index…32

About the Author…32

Time to Celebrate

Switching the calendar to December means it's holiday time! Christmas, Hanukkah, Kwanzaa, and New Year's Day are all holidays to look forward to at the end of each year.

Everyone celebrates the holidays a little bit differently. Your family customs, the region where you live, and your religion may all play a part in the **traditions** you enjoy. You might decorate the halls with Christmas decorations. You might eat potato latkes for Hanukkah or light the kinara for Kwanzaa. You might even stay up until midnight to ring in the New Year!

Families light candles on the menorah during the eight days of Hanukkah.

The holiday season is a time to enjoy parties, games, and feasts. It is also a special time to spend with friends and family. Gifts also play a part in the celebrations. Making crafts is a personal way to share your creative gifts with others.

Many people give gifts during the winter holidays.

WHEN DO YOU CELEBRATE?
Christmas — December 25
Hanukkah — 25th day of the Hebrew month Kislev (in November and/or December)
Kwanzaa — December 26 to January 1
New Year's Eve — December 31
New Year's Day — January 1

The Winter Holidays

The Christmas tree tradition began in Germany.

Christmas

Christmas is a religious holiday. On this day, Christians remember the birth of Jesus Christ more than two thousand years ago. Many Christians and non-Christians enjoy the holiday by giving gifts, singing **carols**, and decorating evergreen trees. Many children await the arrival of Santa Claus, a jolly man from the North Pole who brings gifts while everyone is sleeping.

Hanukkah

Hanukkah is also a religious holiday. This festival of lights lasts for eight days. Jewish people use this time to remember what their religion stands for. During Hanukkah, families light candles in a candleholder called a menorah. It has nine candles, one for each night of the celebration plus one that is used to light all the others.

Kwanzaa

Kwanzaa is much newer than the other major winter holidays. It was first celebrated in 1966 as a way to bring African Americans together as a community. It celebrates ideas such as unity, creativity, helping each other, working together, remembering one's past, and sharing responsibility. To celebrate, families set a table with holiday symbols, such as fruits, corn, a candleholder called a kinara, and a unity cup.

New Year's Eve and New Year's Day

People have been celebrating the New Year for centuries. It wasn't until 1582 that the Western calendar officially made January 1 the start of a new year. Some **cultures** have their own new year celebrations based on their traditional calendars. Many people ring in the New Year late at night on December 31 with parties, feasts, and loud celebrations.

Symbols of the Season

You can **adapt** almost any craft to celebrate any winter holiday. Here are some ideas for symbols and colors that represent each celebration. You can use them to decorate your creations.

Christmas symbols

- Plants such as mistletoe, holly, poinsettias, and evergreen trees
- Candles, stars, and strings of lights
- Candy canes, gingerbread houses, and ribbon candy
- Bells, wreaths, and ornaments
- Santa Claus, reindeer, and a sleigh
- The colors red, green, gold, and silver

Hanukkah symbols

- Dreidel
- Chocolate coins (gelt)
- Star of David
- Menorah and candles
- The colors blue, white, and silver

Kwanzaa symbols

- Straw mat
- African cloth
- Kinara and candles
- Fruit and ears of corn
- Unity cup
- The colors red, black, and green

New Year's Eve and New Year's Day symbols

- Fireworks, horns, and other noisemakers
- Confetti and streamers
- Clocks and calendars
- Father Time and the New Year's Baby
- Parades
- Any colors you like!

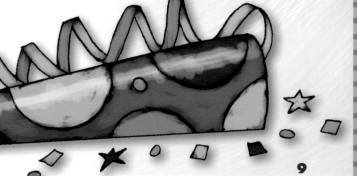

Basic Tools

To make the crafts in this book, you will need a variety of craft supplies. You can find these supplies in craft stores, supermarkets, or hardware stores. You may have many of the supplies around your house already.

Cutting tools
- Paper scissors
- Fabric scissors
- Box cutter or craft knife (Always ask an adult to help when you use a box cutter or craft knife. They are extremely sharp!)

Glue and tape
- White school glue, glue stick, invisible tape (for paper)
- Tacky glue (for craft foam)
- Duct tape (for cardboard)

Papers
- Construction paper
- Aluminum foil
- Craft foam
- Vellum (a **translucent** paper that lets some light through)

- **Adhesive** shelf paper or contact paper (a vinyl sheet that is sticky on one side)

Painting supplies
- Acrylic paint, paintbrushes, paper plate **palette**
- Spray paint (Have an adult help you with spray paint. Always spray it in a well-**ventilated** area. Outside is the best.)
- Newspaper, cardboard, and smock to keep you and your work surface clean.

Other supplies
- Pencil
- Ruler
- Tapestry needle
- Ribbons, bows, bells, beans, and beads
- Fabric scraps, chenille sticks (also known as pipe cleaners), markers, glitter, and stickers
- Wooden skewers and dowels
- Magazines, aluminum cans, toilet paper tubes, cardboard boxes, wire rings, and Styrofoam balls

Ribbon Wreath

Holiday packages come wrapped in ribbons and bows. After the excitement of unwrapping is done, these colorful trimmings often get tossed away. Collect various bows and ribbons and make a wreath that welcomes your friends and family.

Materials

- 12-inch (30-centimeter) wire wreath ring
- 15 to 20 bows
- Ribbons and chenille sticks
- Green curling ribbon cut into 12-inch (30 cm) lengths
- Scissors
- Pencil

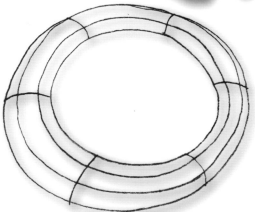

Steps

1. Thread a piece of curling ribbon through some of the loops in the back of a bow.

Then tie the ribbon onto the wreath ring, knotting it in the back.

2. Have an adult curl the ends of the ribbon with a scissors by holding the blade of the open scissors at the base of the ribbon and running the edge of the scissor along the ribbon to the end.

3. Repeat with the rest of your bows. Fit as many as you can onto the wreath. Crowding them together and overlapping them will make your wreath look even better.

4. Fill in any empty spaces on the wreath with smaller bows and ribbons.

5. Twist the chenille sticks onto the frame. Then wrap the ends around a pencil to make a **coil**.

6. Bring all of the curled green ribbons from the back to the front. You can hang your finished wreath from a wreath hook or a nail.

Oversized Dreidel

Families play the dreidel game during Hanukkah. A dreidel is a four-sided top. Each side has a Hebrew letter. Make this oversized dreidel for oversized fun. Just make sure you have enough space to play!

Materials
- Large square cardboard box
- Old broomstick or dowel, about 4 feet (1 meter) long
- Duct tape
- Box cutters or scissors
- Paint and paintbrush
- Permanent marker
- Ruler or tape measure

Steps
1. Remove all the old tape and labels from the box.
2. Cut a triangle from a corner of one of the box's bottom flaps. Make a straight line with a ruler before cutting. Use this triangle to measure equal-sized triangles on all other bottom flap corners. Cut these triangles off. Tape the bottom flaps together.

3. Place the broomstick into the box so it pokes out the bottom end about 10 inches (25 cm). Tape around the stick to hold it in the center. This step is easier with a friend's help.

4. At the top of the box, use a ruler to find the center of each top flap. Cut a 1-inch (2.5 cm) slot in the center of each flap. Close two of the top flaps. Center the stick so that the slots help hold it in place. Tape these flaps closed.

5. Close the other two flaps. Make sure the stick is centered between the slots. Tape these flaps closed. You may need someone to hold the broomstick while you tape.

6. Rip a piece of duct tape in half. Use strips to secure the stick to the box so it won't move.

7. Paint the box to hide any marks or tape. Allow the paint to dry.

8. Draw the Hebrew letters shown here on the sides of your dreidel.

nun   gimel   hay   shin

LET'S PLAY!
Here's how to play the dreidel game.
1. Divide up equally a number of chocolate coins (gelt), nuts, buttons, or other small tokens.
2. Every player adds a token to the center pile.
3. Spin the dreidel. If it lands on:
   (נ): do nothing
   (ג): take the whole pile
   (ה): take half the pile
   (ש): add one to the pile
4. Continue taking turns spinning. If the pile disappears, everyone adds one token. The player who collects all the tokens wins!

Kwanzaa Garland

Garlands are strands of flowers, leaves, or ornaments that people use to decorate for the holidays. A garland in red, green, and black is a perfect decoration for Kwanzaa. Hang garlands on mantels, trees, windows, or doorways.

Materials

- Red, green, and black fabric
  (You don't need much, so scraps work well)
- Fabric scissors
- 12 1.5-inch (4 cm) Styrofoam balls
- Wooden skewers
- White glue
- Black ribbon $\frac{1}{8}$-inch (3 millimeters) wide
- Tape
- 13 small wooden beads
- Tapestry needle

Steps

1. Cut the fabric into strips ¼-inch (6 mm) wide.
2. Carefully poke a Styrofoam ball onto a skewer. Place a generous dot of white glue anywhere on the ball.

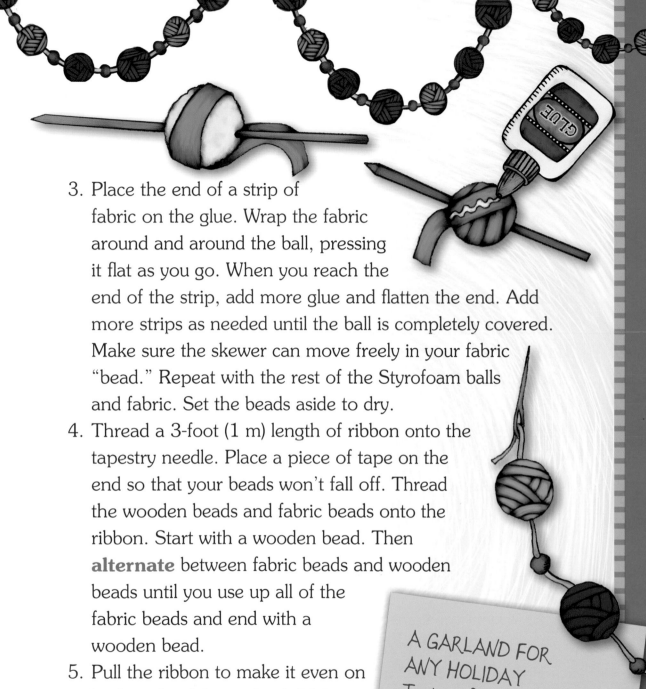

3. Place the end of a strip of fabric on the glue. Wrap the fabric around and around the ball, pressing it flat as you go. When you reach the end of the strip, add more glue and flatten the end. Add more strips as needed until the ball is completely covered. Make sure the skewer can move freely in your fabric "bead." Repeat with the rest of the Styrofoam balls and fabric. Set the beads aside to dry.

4. Thread a 3-foot (1 m) length of ribbon onto the tapestry needle. Place a piece of tape on the end so that your beads won't fall off. Thread the wooden beads and fabric beads onto the ribbon. Start with a wooden bead. Then **alternate** between fabric beads and wooden beads until you use up all of the fabric beads and end with a wooden bead.

5. Pull the ribbon to make it even on both ends of the garland. Make a loop at each end and knot it as close to the beads as you can. Now you have a garland with loops for hanging.

A GARLAND FOR ANY HOLIDAY
To transform this into Christmas garland, make fabric beads in red and green. For Hanukkah, make them blue and white.

Magazine Trees

Evergreen trees stay green even through a cold and snowy winter. Bring some of the outside indoors! Make trees from old magazines or catalogs by folding up the pages. Use them to create a decorative display for any winter holiday. Make a forest of them using different sizes of magazines.

Materials

- Old magazines
- Green spray paint (or any color you choose)
- Newspapers
- White and silver glitter (or other colors you choose)

Steps

1. Start with the cover of the magazine. Fold the top edge to the left edge. Press the **crease** flat.

2. Fold the new top edge toward the left. Press the crease flat.

3. Turn the page. Fold the bottom point upward so it is lined up with the bottom edge. Press flat.

4. Repeat steps 1 to 3 with the rest of the magazine pages.

5. Now it's time to spray paint your tree. Head outside to paint, if possible. If you can't go outside, make sure you cover your work area and spray in a well-ventilated area. It's okay if you don't get inside every flap with the paint. While the paint is still wet, sprinkle the tree with glitter. Set your tree outside, and let it dry completely.

Green Spray Paint

A COLORFUL FOREST
You can also paint your trees gold, silver, or any color you choose to match your other holiday decorations. Imagine a lovely, colorful winter forest!

Frosted Snowflake Mirror

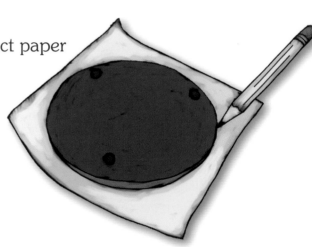

The weather outside might be snowy and cold in December where you live, or it might be sunny and warm. Even if no snowflakes are falling, you can decorate with frosty flakes. This frosted glass snowflake mirror makes a unique decoration for a holiday display.

Materials

- Adhesive shelf paper or contact paper
- 8-inch (20 cm) round mirror
- Pencil
- Scissors
- Newspaper
- White spray paint

Steps

1. Trace the outside of the mirror onto the adhesive shelf paper. Then cut out the circle.
2. Fold the circle in half. Then fold it in thirds.

3. Cut the point off with scissors. Cut a wavy line along the outer edge.

4. Cut a variety of different shapes in different sizes into the folded sides. Be careful not to cut all the way across or put your shapes too close together. You need space in between the cuts to hold your paper together.

5. Unfold your snowflake. Slowly peel off the paper backing. Carefully place your snowflake onto the mirror, sticky side down. Press it flat so that no air bubbles remain.

6. Spray your mirror with spray paint. You only need to make a few light swipes across the surface. Always spray paint outdoors if possible and make sure your workspace is well ventilated. Let your paint dry outside for about 30 minutes.

7. Peel off the adhesive paper to reveal your one-of-a-kind snowflake mirror.

White Spray Paint

Light-Up Lantern

Light plays an important part in many winter holiday decorations. Lights decorate Christmas trees, and candles glow from menorahs and kinaras. Lanterns are a bright way to spread some light in December. Decorate your lantern with symbols that reflect your own holiday traditions.

Materials

- 1 milk or orange juice carton, cleaned well
- Scissors or craft knife
- Black paint and paintbrush
- Pencil
- 4 sheets of vellum paper
- 1 sheet of black paper
- Black permanent marker
- Glue stick
- 24-inch (60 cm) length of ribbon
- Battery-operated tea light

Steps

1. Cut off the top of the carton, and then cut large rectangles into each of the four sides. Leave enough carton to form a frame around each side. To cut out the side rectangles, draw an outline on

each side of the box. Then poke your scissors into the center of the outline and cut from the center out.

2. Paint the sides and bottom of the carton black (or any color you choose).

3. Cut out sheets of vellum the same size as each side of the carton. Place them inside, and trace the shape of the rectangular hole onto the vellum. Remove.

4. Cut out black paper shapes with symbols of the holiday. These need to fit inside the rectangles. Glue the images in place on the vellum and add smaller details with black permanent marker.

5. Swipe a strip of glue at the bottom of each piece of vellum. Press it into the bottom of one of the frames inside the lantern so the side with the black paper faces out. Repeat with the other sides. Then glue the top of each image to the top of each frame.

6. Punch holes along two opposite edges of the top of the carton. Tie one end of the ribbon to each hole so that you have a loop for hanging.

7. Place the tea light in the bottom of your lantern, and hang it.

Foil Wrapping Paper

Gifts can be the best part of the holidays—both the ones you give and the ones you receive! Create embossed wrapping paper that makes your gifts stand out. Embossing is a method of making a raised image on paper.

Materials

- Heavy-duty aluminum foil
- Scissors
- A pencil with a dull tip
- A sheet of craft foam

Steps

1. Cut the aluminum foil to the size you need to wrap your gift. Place it dull side up on top of the craft foam. This will give you a soft surface to press into.
2. Use the pencil to draw shapes, symbols, and designs on the aluminum foil. Press gently so that the pencil does not go through the foil. Continue until you have covered most of the surface with designs.
3. Flip the foil over. All of your drawings will be embossed on the shiny side. Use this paper to wrap a special gift.

Noisemakers and Confetti Cannons

Happy New Year! Many people ring in the New Year with parties, fireworks, music, and lots of noise! Make these noisemakers and confetti cannons to hand out to guests at your New Year's Eve celebration so everyone can join in the fun.

Materials

- 1 empty, clean aluminum soda can
- 1 cardboard toilet paper tube
- Colorful paper and stickers
- Ruler
- Pencil
- Craft foam
- Scissors
- Tacky glue
- Dry white beans
- About 5 small jingle bells
- 12-inch (30 cm) dowel
- Confetti
- Small streamers

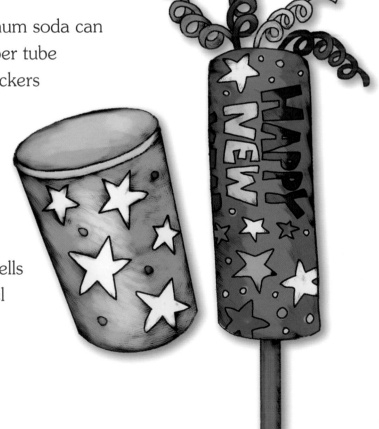

Steps for a noisemaker

1. Cut a strip of paper that is the width of your can and about 12 inches (30 cm) long. Tape it to the side of the can, roll it around the can, and tape the end flat. Decorate it with stickers.

2. Trace the top of the can on a piece of craft foam, and then cut out the circle. Trim the edges until the circle fits snugly in the top of the can. Remove it and set it aside for now.

3. Put a handful of dried beans and the jingle bells inside the can.

4. Glue the foam disc to the top of the can. Once it has dried, you can shake your can to make some noise!

Steps for a confetti cannon

1. Cut a strip of paper the width of the toilet paper tube and about 12 inches (30 cm) long. Tape it to the side of the tube, roll it around the tube, and tape the end flat.

2. Decorate it with stickers.
3. Trace the end of the tube onto a piece of craft foam twice. Cut out the two circles. Trim the edges so that the circles just fit inside the tube.
4. Use the scissors to snip an X shape in the center of one of the circles.
5. Poke the dowel through the X. Push the foam circle to the end of the dowel.
6. Spread glue on top of the circle and dowel. Place the other foam circle on top of the glue, and set it aside to dry.
7. Once the circles are dry, push the circle end of the dowel inside the bottom of the cannon. Load the cannon with small ribbons and confetti from the top.
8. Push the dowel into the tube to shoot out the streamers and confetti!

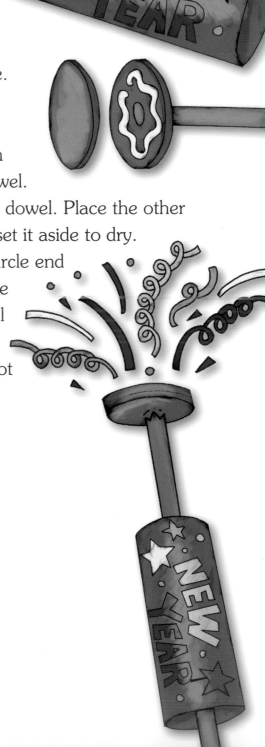

MAKE YOUR OWN CONFETTI
You can buy a bag of confetti to put in your cannon. But you can also easily make your own confetti. Simply collect scraps of paper and cut them up into tiny bits or punch them into circles with a hole puncher.

After the Holidays

How did you join in holiday celebrations this year? Did you dance or sing? Did you play games? Did you help bake treats? When the holidays are over, you may have a lot of cleaning up to do! You may still be full from your holiday meals. You may have gifts to play with. You may be worn-out from all the fun!

Making your own decorations is a great way to join in the celebrations. By making crafts, you've created memories, too. People will appreciate the time you took to make the holidays special. And even though the holidays are over, you can celebrate again next year!

The winter holidays are a great time to spend with family and friends.

Glossary

adhesive (ad-HEE-siv) a substance, such as glue, that makes things stick together

adapt (uh-DAPT) to make something work in a different way or for a different purpose

alternate (AWL-tur-nayt) go back and forth between two things

carols (KAYR-uhlz) joyful songs, especially ones sung at Christmas

coil (KOIL) a loop or series of loops

crease (KREES) a fold or line in fabric or paper

cultures (KUHL-churz) the ideas, customs, traditions, and ways of life of different groups of people

palette (PAL-ut) a flat board that is used for mixing paints

traditions (truh-DISH-uhnz) customs, ideas, or beliefs that are handed down from one generation to the next

translucent (trans-LOO-suhnt) not completely clear like glass, but able to let light through

ventilated (VEN-tuh-lay-tid) allowing fresh air in and stale air out

For More Information

Books

Adler, David A. *The Story of Hanukkah*. New York: Holiday House, 2011.

Cox, Meg. *The Book of New Family Traditions: How to Create Great Rituals for Holidays and Every Day*. Philadelphia: Running Press, 2012.

Groner, Judyth Saypol. *Maccabee Meals: Food and Fun for Hanukkah*. Minneapolis: Kar-Ben Publishing, 2012.

Otto, Carolyn. *Celebrate Kwanzaa*. Washington, D.C.: National Geographic, 2008.

Owen, Ruth. *Christmas Sweets and Treats*. New York: Windmill Books, 2013.

Rissman, Rebecca. *Kwanzaa*. Chicago: Heinemann Library, 2011.

Web Sites

Family Education: Christmas

http://fun.familyeducation.com/holidays/christmas/33097.html
Find ideas for activities, crafts, and fun ways to celebrate Christmas.

History of the Holidays

www.history.com/topics/holidays
Watch videos and read about the history of holidays.

My Jewish Learning

www.myjewishlearning.com/holidays/Jewish_Holidays/Hanukkah.shtml
Learn about how people celebrate Hanukkah.

Index

adhesive paper, 11

Christmas, 4, 5, 6, 8, 17, 22
confetti cannons project, 26, 27–28

dreidels, 14–15

embossing, 24

foil wrapping paper project, 24–25
frosted snowflake mirror project, 20–21

glue, 10

Hanukkah, 4, 5, 7, 9, 14–15, 17, 22

Jesus Christ, 6

kinaras, 4, 7, 9, 22
knives, 10
Kwanzaa, 4, 5, 7, 9, 16–17, 22
Kwanzaa garland project, 16–17

light-up lantern project, 22–23

magazine trees project, 18–19
menorahs, 7, 9, 22

New Year's Day, 5, 7, 9
New Year's Eve, 5, 7, 9, 26
noisemakers project, 26, 27

oversized dreidel project, 14–15

paint, 11
paper, 10–11, 24–25

ribbon wreath project, 12–13

Santa Claus, 6, 8
scissors, 10
symbols, 7, 8, 9, 22

tape, 10
traditions, 4–5, 6, 7, 22

About the Author

Dana Meachen Rau is the author of more than 300 books for children on many topics, including science, history, cooking, and crafts. She creates, experiments, researches, and writes from her home office in Burlington, Connecticut.